WHEN EVERY DAY COUNTS

TERRANCE MASSEY

When Every Day Counts

Copyright (c) 2019 by Terrance Massey

All Rights reserved. No part of this book may be reproduced in any form, stored in a retrieved system, or in any form by any means - electronic, mechanical, photocopy, recording, or otherwise - without prior written permission of the publisher, except as provided by United States of America copyright law.

Unless otherwise indicated, all Scripture quotations are from the King James Version of the Holy Bible.

ISBN 978-1-947741-41-6

Published by Kingdom Publishing, LLC
Odenton, Maryland 21113
www.kingdompublishingllc.com

Printed in the U.S.A.

ACKNOWLEDGEMENTS

There were countless of people who encouraged me to write this book. Time will not permit me to be able to list them all and there isn't enough paper and scrolls that can hold the depths of my gratitude toward each and everyone of them. To you all, I say, "Thank you so much."

I want to acknowledge and thank my Bishop, Antonio Palmer, and his wife, Pastor Barbara Palmer, for their prayers, leadership and love towards me.

I want to thank my lovely wife, Jamie, for your support throughout my reentry into society.

I definitely thank God for keeping me for 10,334 days.

I thank my family for the love they've shown and have given me since I've touched down again in society.

I'd like to give a special shout out of thanks to my church family for being there for me. The prayers and the laughs were much needed and appreciated.

Lastly, I thank my mother and father.

TABLE OF CONTENTS

SECTION I
Life in The Mansion

THE MANSION	1
THE ADOPTION	5
SURVIVAL	9
27 STEPS TO SURVIVE THE MANSION	15
SUICIDE	29
HOSTAGE SITUATION	33
ILLITERACY: IQ OF 52	39
PROFICIENT IN LAW	43
THE STRIKE, MOVEMENT NEEDED TO TAKE PLACE	49
THE RIOT	53
THE SIX COMMON WEAPONS	59

SECTION II
Transition from Islam to Christianity
{In Search of Peace, I Found Jesus}

SOUGHT PEACE	67
MUSLIMS WITH CHRISTIAN HEARTS	71
REJECTION OF THE MUSLIMS AS A CHRISTIAN	79
REPLACING THE QURAN SURAHS WITH BIBLE CHAPTERS & VERSES	85
THE REASONS FOR MY CONVERSION	91
HOW GOD KEPT ME	97

THE MANSION

CHAPTER 1

When I awaken this morning, I knew that the day would be full of mysteries and pain. The night before I was adopted by *the surrogate* at the age of 18. This adoption was a result of my biological parents, who were no longer able to contain or keep me under their control.

For the next 10,334 days, I was going to be raised by the surrogate at "The Mansion." The surrogate had very strict rules and harsh punishments. I was very surprised of the spacious Mansion that I had been placed in. It had a huge yard extending out to acres of land. I had my own bed room and a half bathroom. There was a large dinning room where the chefs prepared large delicious meals. For exercise, there was a basketball court. For entertainment, there was a game room with a Ping Pong table and a Billiards (Pool) table. There were also chauffeurs to drive me around so that I could take care of my business needs. I had the opportunity to meet all types of people from all walks of life and made friends with a few of them. I was kindly provided a therapist to help iron out my differences, without any expenses to me - free of charge. I was also able to attend school as well as receive vocational training while staying at The Mansion.

The Mansion had all these great things and to top it off, it also provided me with a job and medical benefits. Yes, you could say that my surrogate was very wealthy.

But why did I awaken the next morning looking for mysteries and pain? Surely my surrogate was providing me with all my needs. So, why was I feeling so unhappy and hurt? This morning I rose feeling heartbroken, wondering to myself, how could I reverse this adoption? I missed my parents, who didn't have any of these things to offer me like the surrogate had. But as you read on in this book, you will discover, like I did, that things supra do not outweigh love. My surrogate, by no means, loved me whatsoever. I knew this as an incontrovertible fact. It was all about the thirty thousand dollars per year that he collected for my housing.

THE ADOPTION

CHAPTER 2

On December 24, 1982, I was removed from my mother's custody, because it was decided that my conduct warranted placement into The Mansion with my surrogate who would have several eyes watching and monitoring my actions and behavior to keep me on the straight and narrow. The adoption was also made because it was decided that my surrogate could provide me with a formal education since I was not able to read or write - my IQ was only 52. Innately I had been predisposed to a system that said I had an intellectual deficiency and that I was emotionally unbalanced with a learning disability having acute psychotic episodes. Emotionally distraught, I suffered as a man from peer pressure, consumed by exacerbated problems of poverty, being raised by a single parent's drug abuse, along with child abuse mounting with other close calls on my life.

On December 25, 1982, I had awakened to the fact that I was faced with a new life. Despite the adversities I had already faced, life with my surrogate had begun. It was so surreal. In the first thirty days I repeatedly tried to block out the transition in my mind. However, the reality of it all continued to thrust through my denial. I was an emotional wreck, even to the point of being psychotic. I was crying, praying and talking to myself – telling myself how dumb I was for committing the act that led me to this adoption in the first place.

My mind had begun playing tricks on my subconscious, stating that the judge had made a dire mistake and would soon correct this and free me from my bondage. I frequently thought about my family and how much I really missed them. I kept saying to myself, "I just want to go home and be with my family." Every time I cried myself to sleep at night I would say, "I am really at home and this is all a dream." But in the reality of it all, I would open my eyes and find myself gazing up at the high ceiling and the concrete walls that surrounded me. I knew then that my reality was not a dream. It was my living nightmare. I started crying and as the hot saturating tears rolled down my chin I prayed and asked God, "Please do not let this be my end." I had made many calls to my mother pleading that she would come and free me, but I began to realize that there was nothing she or anyone else could do for me.

I had thought at that time that God was punishing me for all my transgressions that I committed against my victim and multiple others. I became angry, bitter and violent. Acting out caused me to get into fights where I had been beaten on three separate occasions by the security guards. At that point, I had convinced myself that I had nothing else to lose. I consequently started fights on purpose. My assaultive behavior was now persistent, continuing into my second, third and fourth month.

Because of this relentless behavior, I was placed on lockdown status twenty three hours per day. I was bitter and calloused against the world and its system. I felt the world had failed me and put me in this predicament. At this point, I felt as though I was an outcast. After eighteen long years, I felt as though I did not fit into what the world considered to be normal. I could not read or write like the others that were in my class. However, with all of this, I felt a bit of relief. I was away from the torment of the physical abuse of my oldest brother and my father. Subsequently, by the fifth month all of that changed and the nightmare started all over again. This time my physical beatings were coming from the security guards of The Mansion and in return I would beat on other residents. I would give them the same beatings that I received. I was taught nothing but violence for most of my unnatural life and the journey that I had acquired was indeed going to be a very violent road that I would eventually travel down. Well, at least those were my thoughts for the next seven thousand and three hundred (7,300) days.

⋯ SURVIVAL

CHAPTER 3

On or about the date of November, Nineteen Eighty-three (1983) - I was only nineteen years old at that time - I realized that I was responsible for being kept in a place filled with drug dealers, pedophiles, rapist, murders and psychotic serial killers. I had to acknowledge that I was responsible for keeping myself alive! I realized that I was in the correct place, because of my transgressions and disobedience to the laws of the land. I cried my last tears and strapped myself in for the ride and stated to myself, "You have to work on surviving in this animalistic environment." So, I taught myself the 27 steps to survive in The Mansion, because my survival was mandatory. I did not want this to be my end. Surely, I did not think that life in The Mansion was going to be that hard. But once I witnessed the many murders, rapes, fights, assaults, robberies and stabbings, I knew that I had a task on my hands.

Many residents here at The Mansion would hang themselves to escape this harsh environment. I laid witness to one of the residents who killed himself by taking sleeping pills. To assist his own demise, he placed a plastic bag over his head and slipped a noose around his neck and hung himself. I guess he thought that he was taking the easy way out, but to me, that was the most difficult way. Besides, the Word of God states that suicide is a murder and to take one's own life is a sin.

I was not affiliated with any type of religion during the first seventy-three hundred (7,300) days of "the adoption." However, I knew that suicide was wrong from the 10 commandments **(Exodus 20:1-17)**[1], all these commandments are to be obeyed. Before the adoption, I never read the Bible, but I ear-hustled it and was able to pick up on a few of the Bible's verses and "Thou shalt not kill." That was one of those prevalent verses. I knew that God existed. I just did not pray, nor did I have a personal relationship with Him.

The reality of me surviving this animalistic environment without aid would be impossible. I was a fighter and survivor by nature. There was a strength that dwelled inside of me to survive this caustic place. My father had taught me survival skills to survive the mean streets of Southeast (S.E.) Washington DC., which in turn aided me some. These certain set of skills inevitably caused my nature to be a murderer and a vicious person, which placed me into The Mansion. So, I had to use my cunningness and skills to survive in this place. I would pray to God to help me through my ordeal. I asked Him to keep me well and of good strength. I asked for His covering over me and that He would guard my mind and keep my sanity for the entire time that I was here in The Mansion. God heard and answered my prayers in full supra. **Matthew 7:7 says,** *"Ask and it shall be given you."* You see, I knew of God, but I did not "know Him." Yet, He still sent His angels to place a hedge of protection around me during my stay.

Endnotes

1   The 10 Commandments are found in the book of Exodus, in the Old Testament of the Bible.

27 STEPS TO SURVIVE THE MANSION

CHAPTER 4

Step 1: Prayer
Step 2: Observe
Step 3: Stay Alert
Step 4: Watch Your Back
Step 5: Do Not Get to Know A Lot of the Residence
Step 6: Learn Everyday Routine
Step 7: Wear Underwear in the Shower
Step 8: Learn your Roommates Rules
Step 9: Avoid Direct Eye Contact in the Kitchen
Step 10: Avoid Letting Your Eyes Drop in the Shower
Step 11: Always Defend Yourself
Step 12: Put Forth an Effort to Avoid Fights
Step 13: If the Telephone is Hung Upside Down, Do Not touch it
Step 14: If You Make a Transaction Fulfill it
Step 15: Do Not borrow 2 For 1's
Step 16: Attend Whatever Program that are Offered
Step 17: Attend Church
Step 18: Do Not be a room Hog
Step 19: Be Clean
Step 20: Keep Room Clean
Step 21: Do Not Love Television more than freedom
Step 22: Do Not Argue Over the Microwave
Step 23: Be Patient While Waiting at the Gate
Step 24: When your Door is Hit, Get to it Immediately
Step 25: In the Yard Workout
Step 26: If the Walk to the Dinning Room is Quiet, "Watch Out!"
Step 27: After Using the Toilet Wipe it Down and When You Wash Your hands, Wipe out the Sink

Prayer

Clearly prayer is how you speak to God. Jeremiah 33:3 says, *"Call unto Me and I will answer thee and shew thee great and might things, that thou knowest not."*[1] The Word of God also says in Colossians 4:2, *"Continue in prayer and watch in the in the same with thanksgiving."*[2] 1Thessalonians 5:17 also says, *"Pray without ceasing."*[3] In Proverbs 15:29, the Word of God states, *"The Lord is far from the wicked: but he heareth the prayer of the righteous."*[4]

When I began to pray regularly, God would fully answer my prayers. Plus, the prayers would strengthen me and I truly believed that God was going to grant my prayers. The Word states in Mark 11:24, *"Therefore I say unto you, What things soever ye desire, when ye pray, believe that ye receive them, and ye shall have them."*[5] Prayer gave me peace in my life and kept me sane.

Observe

You must study people and the atmosphere around you. In learning the characteristics and personalities of the residence, you get a better picture of the attitudes and habits of the men you are around. With this observation, you can deal with and stay away from them. You see, this step is very important, because if you become friends with a troublemaker, you will not make it home. You could also end up going back to court having to answer to another added offense, receiving extra time onto your sentence. Additionally, if you don't observe your associates closely, you might end up with someone you come to terms with and have to end up having to fight or destroy them.

Stay Alert

In The Mansion, things sometimes happen so quickly around you that you did not really realize that they were in progress. You could walk into the middle of a situation in progress and lose your life, because you were not paying attention. When you are anywhere inside The Mansion, you must stay alert. There were multiple times when there was either a stabbing taking place or someone was being robbed. Many fellas were in there who were not aware of the crimes that was taking place around them. There was an incident where a buddy of mine was about to walk into the middle of these two dudes having "a beef" (altercation). Fortunately, he was called out to come back.

Watch Your Back

Guys will sneak up on you while walking to the gym, the yard or the dinner hall, etc. They would split your head open or stab you to death. I have witnessed many dudes slipping and eventually lost their lives. I used to continually watch my own back and expected anything to happen at any time. Particularly, in the tunnel, on the stairs, out of the view of the guards, The Mansion was spacious with dark corners and blindspots where the guards were not able to see.

Do Not Get to Know A lot of the Residence
The Mansion held thousands of men with all different types of personalities. The more people you were familiar with, the more trouble you could get yourself into and the more beefs you will have; the more arguments you could find yourself in.

Learn Everyday Routine
It was very important to learn just how The Mansion operated, how it was run. Learnig how it ran will help you survive. Simply just walking to dinner is an ordeal. You could get your life snuffed out, because you were unprepared when your door opened. When your door opens for dinner be ready. You never know if somebody is going to try and run up in your cell to rub, stab or murder you. So it is very important to know and learn your times when certain events take place.

Wear Underwear in the Shower
There is a large assembly of men in The Mansion that are into other men. The straight men are gay bias and will not get in the shower with other man, even when there are six showers to a shower room. The rule in the shower is that you must wear your underwear in the shower. Otherwise you are labeled as a "Pack faggy" or

homosexual.

Learn Your Roommates Rules

In The Mansion, when you are placed in the room with another guy who has already had that room for some time, you must come into that room already knowing that you must respect his rules and regulations of that cell. If not, you will end up fighting to the death. Example: he might have two or more specific rules about wiping down the toilet seat after doing your business. He could also want you to clean the room a certain way on "Clean Day."

Avoid Direct Eye Contact in the Kitchen

In The Mansion, any type of direct eye contact could be an invitation to a fight, especially when you are at dinner. This is where that threat is heightened. Someone is bound to take that the wrong way as you are either plotting on their life, seeking trouble with someone or you are just plain gay and looking for a hook up. Either one of these could get you killed.

Avoid Letting Your Eyes Drop in the Shower

There is a lot of homosexual men in The Mansion and most of them are on the "down-low". If your eyes drop in the shower and you are caught doing it—more than likely you will be labeled as a queer. However, if you come back in the shower and do it again to someone else, more than likely you could end up dead.

Always Defend Yourself

There in The Mansion you must always stay on high alert like "Home Security," because you are in an environment where there are ten (10) prominent ways that murder can be implemented at any time. Dudes in The Mansion are already on the edge, for the most part, suffering from high anxiety, antagonism, depression and complex post-traumatic stress disorder (C- PTSD). A percentage of them are walking, talking, ticking time bombs ready to go off at any given moment. It is that very same reason why the homicide rate is so very high inside The Mansion.

Put forth an effort to Avoid Fights

There can be so many conflicts in The Mansion that you can end up seriously hurt or possibly dead. Ultimately, you try to weigh both sides of the matter where you and the other guy are involved. There is no real rationalization to the matter, that either way could end badly. So, from the very beginning you must choose your battles so you can live another day. Because once a bitter conflict starts and turns physical, more than likely, here, inside The Mansion, it will be grave bound.

If the Phone is Turned Upside Down, Don't Touch It

In The Mansion, telephones are a privilege and whenever a privilege is given, someone always find a way to abuse that privilege. For instance, everyone is given a privilege time to use the phone. However, some guys want to use their time and yours too. I called these guys, "Phone Hoggers." They would use the phone until their time would end and then hang the phone upside down on the community commercial phone hook that hung on the wall. If you picked up the phone to use it, you were asking for trouble. It was kill or be killed at that point.

If You Make a Transaction, Fulfill it

There are guys in The Mansion that run little "Stores" and lend to the hungry. They call it a "2-for-1," earning a 100% profit from the borrowers. There is also another type of transaction where you exchange a store item for a dinner meal. Most of the guys in The Mansion usually wanted more chicken. So, if a guy agrees to give up his portion of chicken next meal, in turn, he was then paid with a box of Little Debbies for his chicken portion. But then the very next day they serve chicken, that same guy rethinks the deal that he made and eats the agreed upon chicken portion that he originally promised and got paid for with the box of Little Debbies, which by the way, has eaten the whole box of Little Debbies as well. The least to say, is that I have seen people badly beaten because of reneging on their transaction.

Do Not borrow 2-For-1s
Basically, stay away from borrowing 2-for-1s, because they will hurt your pockets and cause conflicts. This is due to the fact that guys depend on their family to send them money to go to the "Store." But then something happens and they do not receive the awaited money from their family. The lender does not want to hear any excuses why you do not have his items on the day that was promised. There are 2 things that could happen in this scenario. The first scenario, he charges you 3-for-1 the next time there's a transaction at the "Store." The second and worst scenario, he bust you in the head or hit you up.

Attend Whatever Programs that are Offered
The Mansion will offer vocational education and job skill trainings. It is imperative that you participate therein. It keeps your mind focus and out of trouble. This also gives you a chance to prepare you for a brighter future. The psychology and therapy programs are life savers.

Attend Church
Spiritual growth is a very important element when surviving in The Mansion. The devil is busy and will manipulate and twist people's minds, causing them to become lost and turned out souls. Therefore, you must

have the Lord in your life. You must allow your mind to stay focused on the Word of God, praise the Lord daily and give thanks - for He is worthy of the praise. God and God alone is your only salvation. He is the only one to set your shackles free and release you from the torment of the devil.

Do Not be a Room Hog

In The Mansion, there are two men to a room. The room has one toilet and one sink. It is called, "A Half Bath." Your door is usually locked for your own protection. Your door is opened for meals, showers, workout and store visits. You and your roommate will need to have time alone, you know, without the other one always being around in the room. So, go out to the yard or the Rec Hall.

Be Clean

Showers are available everyday at The Mansion. If you miss a couple of showers you are labeled as a dirty person.

Keep your Room Clean

It is very important to keep your room clean, because it reflects your general hygiene and if you don't it causes a lot of problems for you in The Mansion.

Do Not Love TV More Than Freedom
The one-eyed monster, i.e. the TV, can get you murdered in The Mansion's Rec Hall. To every Rec Hall there are 60 men. Everyone wants to watch something different on this one TV. Feelings get involved, arguments happen, and fights break out. Stabbings would happen or people would get hit in the head with socks that have metal locks inside of them. Nothing good comes out of that. Many men do not make it home because of the TV.

Do Not Argue over the Microwave
In The Mansion, there is one microwave to every 60 men. Everyone would stand in line to use it. Some men would attempt to route you. You need to make your stand or you will be taken advantage of every time.

Be Patient While Waiting at the Gate
At The Mansion there are many security gates. They sometimes take their time opening the gates just to get a response out of you. You need to be patient and wait so you will not get written up, which will make your stay there longer.

When your Door is Hit, Get to it Immediately
When the door to your room is electric and security can open it at any given time, without you expecting it, get to it immediately. Plenty of guys can get your

door opened by lying to security and then run down into your room and stab you.

In the Yard Workout
You get to workout everyday in the yard at The Mansion and it is imperative that you stay in physical shape at The Mansion, because when problems arrive (and they will at The Mansion), you need to be physically fit to deal with any problems you need to contend with.

On the walk to the Dinning Hall and it is Quiet, Watch Out!
The walk to the dining room can be a dangerous one at The Mansion. This is where a man can be stabbed for having a beef with another man. Usually when someone is being hit up or beefing, it gets very quiet.

After Using the Toilet Wipe it Down and When You Wash Your hands, Wipe out the Sink
It is an unwritten law in your room that you are sharing with your roommate. It is imperative to maintain a clean room. Always wipe the seat of the toilet off after use and always wipe out the sink after you wash your hands. This is to maintain the peace with your bunk buddy. Many guys will seriously hurt you for not doing so.

Endnotes

1	Jeremiah 33:3, *"Call unto Me and I will answer thee and shew thee great and might things, that thou knowest not."*

2	Colossians 4:2, *"Continue in prayer and watch in the in the same with thanksgiving."*

3	1 Thessalonians 5:17, *"Pray without ceasing."*

4	Proverbs 15:29, *"The Lord is far from the wicked: but he heareth the prayer of the righteous."*

5	Mark 11:24, *"Therefore I say unto you, What things soever ye desire, when ye pray, believe that ye receive them, and ye shall have them."*

...SUICIDE

CHAPTER 5

With some men's release date in The Mansion, with all its perks, one would think that guys would fight to get in, not die to get out. There were many good men who took the "Road of No-return." Some call the road, "The easy way out." I call it, "The hard way out." Taking one's own life is hard.

I observed a man take his own life by hanging. He did it because he thought he could not live in The Mansion away from his family and loved ones for a long time. He ended his own life by his own hand in the privacy of his own room. Security investigated the death and officially determined it as a suicide. I knew freedom wasn't coming for me through the means of suicide. I was the unwilling witness of many suicides.

Another resident killed himself over a woman. He was a young man, perhaps in his early twenties. The beginning of the end started with him on the phone in the recreation room talking with his girlfriend on the phone. Suddenly, an argument ensued. I was not privy to what the woman on the other end of the line had said, but I heard the young man. With the thrill of defeat in his voice, he asked her, "So, is it over?" He pleaded with her, but to no avail. The call ended. It seemed as though the woman who was on the other end of the phone conversation was tired of waiting for this young man to come home. As he departed the recreation room, I asked him, "Are you, all right?" He answered, "Yeah." But he really wasn't all right. When the recreation room closed and I crossed the corridors, I passed the young man's room. To my horror, he was hanging from the light.

This young man was an upstanding, decent man. The woman must have been a very special young lady. Here's the thing, and there's no getting around it. When you are a resident at The Mansion, family and friends may cut you off, as if you were no longer in existence. Personal visits, phone calls and letters serve as hope, to get the resident of The Mansion through trying times.

This next suicide was committed by a young man who couldn't stand being here at The Mansion. He was in his room. He tied a plastic bag around his head and placed a noose around his neck. He set up on his bed and fell asleep. He was found the next morning, deceased.

Another suicide committed at The Mansion was done by a slitting and slashing of the arm. It was a very slow death by bleeding out.

Another way of committing suicide at The Mansion is called a suicide mission. This is where one goes around taking all challenges and being a bully. For many years, I was on a suicide mission and several times I came very close to my demise. One of those crazy times I was in the District of Columbia (DC) and in Baltimore where I got into a beef. Knives came into play, but God protected me. He saw fit to allow me to be protected by His angels.

This one murder-suicide in The Mansion kind of stuck with me. This one was by handgun. It was done by one of the security guards at The Mansion. He brought in a handgun and shot a lieutenant and then killed himself.

HOSTAGE SITUATION

CHAPTER 6

There were many relationships in The Mansion - forbidden relationships. Relationships between security guards and the residents were not permitted, but love has its way of breaking through policies and rules. The two participants were a teacher and a resident of The Mansion. They became involved with one another. Feelings sparked secretly and love letters were passed. I became the transporter, sneaking letters from the male resident to the female teacher.

One day I was given a letter from the female teacher and an unfamiliar look appeared on her face. It was very strange. It appeared that it wasn't a good letter, because of her expression. Later, I handed the letter to the resident and walked away. I went on with my day. One hour later, I left my room. I was headed back to school for evening classes. The resident approached me and asked me could I transport a letter to the teacher. The expression and the look on his face wasn't a good one at all. But I took the letter to her. I handed it to her and walked away.

After our class had ended, the female teacher handed me another letter and told me not to accept more letters from the male resident. Wow! When I gave him the letter, then relayed the verbal message, he got very angry. As I walked away, I thought to myself, "This concludes our transactions." However, the next time I exited my room for evening classes, he approached me once more. He handed me a final letter. I looked at him, and I asked him, "Man didn't she tell you no more letters?" He made an attempt to justify his disregard of her request. At this time, I had been housed at The Mansion for over 10 years. I witnessed this type of conduct in other forbidden relationships. However, this letter that I read, wow, it was some threatening words in it. So, I decided not to pass this letter to her. Rather, for her safety, I did tell her that he said it's not over and for her to call him to the school – that would be a bad decision.

She went against my advice and called him down to the school to put the matter to rest. Before he left, he came to my room and handed me an envelope with her letters, and I believe the three cassette tapes. He asked me to mail the items off if anything happened. That made bells go off in my head. I wanted to inform The Mansion security, but that was considered snitching and snitching wasn't allowed in The Mansion. So, I listened to the tapes and I read the letters. All I can say was, "Wow!"

In the beginning she was madly in love with him even though she was married. After a few months they had sexual contacts. She felt guilty and wanted to break it off. She did not want to lose her job. But he felt it was too late for that now. He was in love with her and was asking her to leave her husband at this point, because he couldn't stand for her to be with anyone else. The tapes and letters showed the incriminating contents.

He went to the school. A couple of hours later I heard the fire trucks, ambulance, and police cars. Security told us that all traffic was stopped in The Mansion due to a hostage situation at the school. I couldn't believe what I was hearing. I thought about the items, of which, I immediately destroyed. Security informed us that a teacher was being held at knife point. They would not tell us who was involved, but I already knew who it was.

I felt horrible for the both of them. However, they both made their own decisions. She broke The Mansion's policies and rules, and her marriage vows. He, too, broke the policies and rules. Instead of enjoying the ride, he became too involved. He allowed his feelings to get involved in the forbidden love.

Luckily, after a few hours, he gave himself up. Security informed us that the hostage situation was over. I found out later that he did not mention to the police about the illicit affair. He accepted the charge of kidnapping along with other charges. She took a few days off and then returned to work. She was aware that I knew the details of her relationship with the male resident. When she saw me, she was always nice, but she was now worried knowing that I had information that could destroy her marriage and her career. I told her that my lips were sealed. She thanked me. She told me, "I am so relieved." She was the same teacher who taught me English and other subjects. She was the teacher who inspired me to get my diploma.

ILLITERACY/ IQ OF 52

CHAPTER 7

Before the adoption and my placement in The Mansion, I was a bad child in school. I stayed in trouble. Therefore, I was referred to have a psychiatric analysis. The psychiatrist and psychologists diagnosed me as being illiterate. The diagnosis was that I would never be able to read or write. Over the years, that diagnosis germinated in my mind. I was getting into trouble because of that diagnostic opinion. When a teacher would ask me to read, I was ashamed that I couldn't read. I was embarrassed because of what other students might think of me. I'd rather say that I could not read or I would simply say, "No." My illiteracy would cause me to beat up three teachers for saying things like, "That's why you can't read," or "You will never be able to read if you don't try."

I was diagnosed with an IQ of 52. I used to feel inadequate and thought I was stupid and just a waste of sperm. I lived my entire life thinking as such. My own family used to tease me, calling me stupid. My vocabulary was limited, I was quiet and of few words. Mostly, I used profanity to express myself. I was angry most of the time. I turned to drugs and alcohol in the hope of smothering my illiteracy. Unfortunately, all that drugs and alcohol did was compounded the problem. I was then diagnosed with intellectual deficiency and emotional imbalance. This diagnosis was discovered after the adoption and placement into The Mansion.

In The Mansion, education was offered for 1825 days. I felt that I was stagnant because of that simple diagnosis. It haunted my brain and I believed what the doctors said was true. I felt and believed that it was no need to participate in the educational program. I could not read and probably would never be able to write either. I thought to myself, "Why even try?"

In the first 1825 days, I continued my drug and alcohol abuse, desperately attempting to feel better about my situation – the adoption and the illiteracy. It wasn't until one of my buddies pulled me aside and said to me, "Massey, you need to stop running around here doing the same things that got you into The Mansion. Go to school and find peace or else you will not make it out of this joint alive."

I rejected that advice, but later took it under advisory. Two days later, I signed up for school. I was accepted into the educational program. I began on the first-grade level, learning two and three-letter words. I was embarrassed. It took me 1825 days to overcome the doctor's diagnosis. After 3650 days, I received my diploma. Prior to that, I was taking vocational trades six-month courses. Just to name a few, plumbing, carpentry, electric, welding, building trades and auto mechanics.

I earned my eighth-grade certificate which aided me in killing that ill-fated diagnosis the doctors had put in my head. The vocational trades gave me the confidence and the proof that those doctors were so wrong.

In school, I met a lot of guys who were just like me, unable to read and write. Many of them gave up. They simply did not have the strong desire or hunger to achieve a diploma. After I received my diploma, I completed many more skill classes. I received many more skill certificates in relationship classes and classes such as Thinking for Change and MCE Cares. I mentored youth at The Mansion under a social worker, drug program adviser and licensed plumber, and took three computer courses and social skills classes, etc.

Here is my advice to anyone who cannot read or write, "It is just temporary and never permanent. You have to push yourself to get over your defeatist attitude. Accomplish a small goal, setting the diploma as a long-term goal." If I can do it, you can too. Do not let anyone tell you that you cannot achieve anything, especially doctors. They have no idea of the potential you really have on the inside of in you.

PROFICIENT IN LAW

CHAPTER 8

In The Mansion, there were double standards. I was ordered to follow and obey the rules and regulations set forth by my surrogate, or otherwise I would be punished. I was punished for my transgressions on many occasions. My surrogate refused to follow the policies and would get away with it.

After I became educated, I vowed I would be the one who disciplined my surrogates and security staff. I studied law for 5,475 days. I was sometimes called, "Johnny A. Howard" (he was a county judge). He conceded in one of my court presentations that "Massey, in my 30 years on the bench, you put on the best presentation that I have ever seen. Lawyers go to school for years to obtain what you demonstrated here today." I received a court applause.

In one of my other court presentations, another judge in Annapolis City Court, complimented me on my petition. He asked, "Did you do this yourself?" I replied, "Yes Sir." "You did a very good job," was his response. I filed many other petitions, motions, and briefs. My work could be found in caselaw, Massey vs. State; Massey vs. Rosenblatt; Massey vs. Henneberry; Massey vs. Nero; Massey vs. Department of Public Safety.

I guess you have probably figured out by now, that The Mansion I have been referring to is prison.

My surrogate was the secretary of public safety and correctional services. The security, I referred to, was correctional officers. And the adoption was when I was removed from my mother's house and placed in prison for the rest of my natural life. However, all but 40 years was suspended. That equates to 14,600 days. I served 28 years and one month. That is, 10,334 days. It was nothing but the Lord who brought me out of that prison with an education. He brought me out with a new mindset. He brought me out with a sane and sound mind, just as he had done for Peter, Paul, and Joseph as recorded in the Holy Bible.

 I remember I was asked to represent guys in disciplinary hearings. I accepted the offer. I would charge the guys anywhere from $10.00 to $60.00 dollars and upwards depending on the severity of the charges they faced. Disciplinary hearing occurs when a correction officer writes an infraction for violation of a prison rule. The hearing occurs in a court-like setting. The plaintiff is afforded the due process in accordance with the 14th amendment of the Constitution of United States of America.

 One time, I was charged with an escape from a work release facility. There I received an infraction. The captain of the facility liked my wife. He wanted me out of the way. Therefore, he trumped up a false charge of escape against me. The hearing was conducted by a very close friend of the captain. I motioned for postponement until the following week. I knew that the scheduled hearing officer would not be as fair as a lieutenant. The following week, another hearing was scheduled. I motioned for another postponement. I was aware that the new hearing officer would be as equally prejudiced as the first. The third week, another hearing was scheduled. The captain's best friend, another lieutenant, whom I foreknew would be biased, was to be the presiding hearing officer. I motioned for yet another postponement. This time my motion was denied. The hearing officer said, "We are going to get this over with today." The hearing officer admonished me to "fight it on appeal." The statement was made prior to the commencement of the hearing and affirmed my suspicions. I was deemed guilty prior to the proceedings.

By the standards set forth in State law and prison regulations, the hearing simply wasn't fair. It was not an impartial hearing, because the presiding hearing officer made a decision that was not based on evidence. The standard of review is for a disciplinary hearing decision to be based upon substantial evidence. Substantial evidence is evidence which is relevant, and of which reasonable minds might accept as adequate to support a conclusion. I later appealed the decision to the Circuit Court by way of judicial review. I requested a copy of the transcript tape from the prison. I informed the Lieutenant that I would like a copy of the transcript tape as evidence to appeal his decision. The prison officials lied to me by claiming the tape was destroyed. Their conduct was an attempt to deprive me of the most important part of the record, i.e. the tape. The Court of Special Appeals of Maryland ordered the prison to produce the tape within 30 days. Miraculously, the tape was brought back to life and produced by the prison within the 30-day timeframe.

The transcript was reviewed by the court of special appeals. The court overturned the hearing officer's decision, finding that I should not have been found guilty of escape, but only of a failure to return to the facility within one hour of time due. This was my argument from the beginning. The punitive sanction was removal from the work release program, for six months. In lieu of being imprisoned for an additional 14 years, which is a far more severe disciplinary action, essentially because the prison guard was mad at me for exercising my right to appeal. This was arbitrary and capricious and it was an unlawful decision.

Most of the offenses adjudicated by the disciplinary hearing officer were personal in nature rather than legal. Many of the officers embellished the truth, or outright lied, when they wrote infractions or tickets. They clearly violated the executive orders, division of correction DCD 50-2. The officers seemingly operated with impunity. However, when I started winning cases and appeal proceedings, they transferred me from one prison to the next. It didn't matter to me, because one prison was just like the other. They were all the same thing. I have been in many of them, and I still legally whipped them.

THE STRIKE, MOVEMENT NEEDED TO TAKE PLACE

CHAPTER 9

Because of the unjust acts of the officers and the administration, the population organized and executed a solidarity strike. The strike consisted of work and school stoppages and a hunger strike. We refused to talk as we walked. Some of the kitchen workers participated in the strike, but others did not. Therefore, as a deterrent, we poured water in the backs of their TVs and radios, hoping this would sway their participation, but to no avail. Those "Butt-biters" still refused to strike. Therefore, we turned up the heat. Desperate times calls for desperate measures. We put hands on them. We beat them down. The beatings were so severe that out of concern for the holdout kitchen workers, the authorities ordered their work stoppage.

    The strike crippled the facility for four days. The authorities were forced to bring in contract cooks and kitchen workers. Even so, the striking population refused to eat any of the food. As part of our strategic planning, we used the US Postal Service, first informing family and others not to visit during the strike. We also leaked our plight and intention to strike to the local news media outlets. The media found our story newsworthy. Members of the press sought answers from the prison administrative staff. The prison officials downplayed the strike, explaining that certain prisoners were upset over not having ice-coolers on the tiers. They deceptively hid the real reasons for the strike – mistreatment of the inmates at the hand of prison administrators and staff.

The prison administrator – those traders – ultimately called for a meeting between the prison staff and the striking inmates. The striking prisoners held signs out of their windows. The signs informed the media that the explanation provided by prison administrators was merely pretext. We informed them that the administration continuously violated the constitutional rights, human rights and civil rights of the inmates. We were literally tired of their foolishness, so we went on strike. By striking, we hit them where it hurt the most – in their wallets. By striking, we shut down their business – the plantation (in its newest form).

At first, we did not think that it would work, but we knew something had to be done. As men, we had reached the pinnacle of disgust. After the first day, we framed our demands which we would accept from the administration. The administration established an Inmate Administrative Committee (IAC). We presented this idea to the prison population. The meeting occurred one month later. However, in the interim, IAC was permitted to visit every tier in the prison and talk with the prisoners and solicit their complaints. Because of the strike, the quality of the food significantly improved and coolers were put on each tier. There was betterment in the release process.

The correctional officers and prison staff showed respect to the inmates. The prisoners began to receive much needed health and comfort items i.e., food, cosmetic packages, and more.

THE RIOT

CHAPTER 10

In some circles in American society, a dispute or grievance is often called, "a beef," which I referred to earlier in this book. In the prisons, someone (or group) seemingly always had a beef. Some beefs are worse than others. The worse beef in my memory was when warring factions engaged in combat. A national gang known as the "Bloods" established an ominous presence in the prison. They contended with another gang known as the "Black Guerilla Family (BGF)." The BGF had the backing of another gang, "Dead Man Incorporated (DMI)," which consisted mostly of the Caucasian population.

These opposing factions were all beefing tension in the air for about a week. The correctional officers understood something bad or unpleasant was going to happen. They caught wind of the ensuing threat either by the prison grapevine or by preparatory gang activity. Because of the threatening inauspicious tension, they preemptively cancelled Yard activity for the preceding week.

One day, the prison warden uncharacteristically allowed Yard activity. I am suspicious that the warden perhaps had ulterior motives. The warden had augmented his usual security force with extra armament, canine dogs, State Troopers and TACT Teams. The Bloods, BGF, and DMI, as well as the general population had staged makeshift weapons on the prison yards prior to the prison-imposed restricted use. I did not want to show up at a knife fight and everybody had a knife but me. I carried my own knife to the Yard. When there is a beef in the prison, we all carried knives irrespective of whether we were beefing or not.

The day the warden reopened the yard, as predictable, it did not take long before things escalated and the factions violently engaged one another. Initially, in the small yard DMI attacked and repeated stabbing a black man. The man allegedly shot up the home and killed a cousin of one of the DMI members. The man's RAP buddy, a Muslim, pulled his own knife and quickly came to the man's defense. Other Muslims engaged DMI. In the instant, Muslims fight against DMI and BGFs.

Meanwhile, in the big Yard, tensions between factions are nearing the boiling point. The members are anxiously standing by waiting for the call to action; the call to attack their enemies. But then, it was the correctional officers who made the call over the radio, "It's going down!!!" And indeed, the situation quickly got out of the control of the prison correctional officers. One, two, three, four shots of teargas were fired in the small Yard. When the correctional officers moved into action in the small Yard, the awaiting gangs moved to action in the big Yard. A young dude from BGF hit a Blood member with a baseball bat. However, the Blood member managed to grab hold of and arrest the bat from the young man. He then chased the young man across the big yard and all hell broke loose. The correctional officers quickly lost control of the situation as if they ever had control. The bullhorns blared at the all-male population in the Yard, "Get on the Ground!" Despite these repeated commands the bats were wailing and the knives were swinging. The prisoners knew, acquiescence to the correctional officers' commands, to get on the ground, would equate to surrendering one's own life.

None of the inmates complied with the demands of the correctional officers. Then we heard, one, two, three, four, five shots of teargas lobbed into the big Yard. The Cops, State Troopers, and TACT Teams and then the canines were deployed in both prison yards. Their demands were to be taken seriously with no room for misinterpretation. "Get Down, Now! Spread Your Legs and Your Arms Outward! Don't Look Up! Noncompliance is a sign of aggression! We will act as such!!!" There was 100% compliance in the big Yard.

Back in the small Yard everyone was searching for fresh air. The small Yard was enclosed with surrounding buildings. The only way to see out is to look upwards to the sky. There wasn't much air coming in on that fateful hot day. As such, the teargas could not readily escape.

In the big Yard, one by one, on command, the prisoners were ordered from the ground to a stance where they were cuffed and escorted to their tiers and dorms. The prison was in a lockdown status for weeks following the riot. We were forced to eat bag-lunches only.

Thereafter, the TACT Team reappeared at the prison. This time they came to perform a major shakedown. A shakedown is an unannounced prison-wide search for any contraband, including weapons, drugs and paraphernalia, unauthorized phones, food, clothing, etc. The TACT Team executed the shakedown with extreme prejudice. Nothing was regarded as sacred or sentimental. The inmates were stripped searched. The Dorm cells were ransacked. Personal items were thrown everywhere. Contrary to prison policy, nothing was returned to the place where the officers found them. The shakedown was in retribution of the riot. The prison remained in lockdown status even after the shakedown. Prisoner movement required that the prisoners traveled with their hands on their head. This was true even of medical patients. The prison had to regain control over the inmates and the control it lost during the riot. Supra. After a month or so, lockdown was lifted and inmate privileges were restored.

THE SIX COMMON WEAPONS

CHAPTER 11

In prison, there were many injuries that resorted in death. You had to expect that anything could happen in these walls. I had seen my share of things in my twenty-eight (28) years of imprisonment.

There is the unfortunate story of a man who had been stabbed under his left arm with an ice pick. The wound he received from that was the result of his untimely death. What happened was a bully, my homeboy from "the District," who was nice with his hands, used to hit another one of my buddies from Baltimore, MD, showing off his skills. You see, most of the B-more brothers were not skilled with their hands but would fight you and wrestle. They were good at doing that, but would sling a knife if it was called for. My DC buddy went to a B-more buddy and called him out for a fight. The B-more dude was drinking some hot scolding coffee and ended up throwing it on the DC dude's face. Immediately, the B-more dude pulled out an ice pick and chased the DC dude through the dorm. They were leaping on and over bunks and other dudes, until finally, the B-more dude stabbed the DC dude under his left arm and killed the DC dude.

In another case, the weapon was a coffee pot with boiling water in it. Again, there were two men who were in an argument. I believe this one was over a TV. One wanted to watch sports while the other wanted to watch a movie. The "Sports Man" was a pretty big dude. The "Movie Man" knew it was going to be difficult to put him down. So, "Movie Man" let the "Sports Man" (along with his other standbys) win the argument. But when the "Sports Man" fell asleep, "Movie Man" put on a show of his own. He went over to the coffee pot and filled it up with water and plugged it in to let the water boil until it was scorching hot. "Movie Man" then unplugged it and brought the pot and creeped over to the big "Sports Man" bunk and dumped the whole pot of scorching water on the "Sports Man." The "Sports Man" jumped up rubbing his face. His skin was coming off into his hands!

The third choice of weapon is the lock in the sock. This is a unique weapon because of how the lock is placed into the sock. The very heavy part of the lock goes to the bottom of the sock first because of the lock being bottom heavy. Now the incident with the lock-n-sock weapon was an argument which ensued over a commissary item, a 2-for-1. I had mentioned what a 2-for-1 was in a previous chapter. The borrower told the lender, "I am not giving you two back, here is the one that I borrowed." The lender explained to the borrower that when he came and borrowed the commissary, he told him something far different. He went on to explain to the borrower that he was aware that he ran a store and everything is 2-for-1. Thus, if he did not amend to their agreement, then he will consider that the borrower took from him. The borrower said, "If that is what you want to consider, then so be it." The lender said, "Ok fine, say no more." When chow time came, the lender hit the borrower in the back of the head twice with the lock-n-sock. The borrower went straight into shock and walked up to the police. The C/O just looked at him. The borrower was not saying a thing. The borrower was seriously wounded. Blood was gushing profusely out of the back of his head.

The fourth weapon was the homemade butcher knife. One of my buddies got into an ordeal with a young DC boy over the microwave. "DC" hit him in the mouth and busted my buddy's lip wide open. My buddy backed up because the C/O was coming. We all left and went into the recreation hall as though nothing had happened. The "DC boy" was feeling himself. He thought that he had been victorious and had his chest puffed out. The "DC boy" stood over on the other side of the recreation hall looking over at my buddy as if he was proud of the work he had just done on him. But this young buck did not realize that he just messed up and hit the wrong dude in the mouth. My buddy eventually caught up with the "DC boy," (he had been slipping). On that day, my buddy put two butcher knives into that young boy, one into one side and the other one into the other side. DC went stumbling into the grill where the C/O sits and collapsed there.

The fifth weapon of choice is the Jack Mackerel

in the can when it is placed into a pillow case. Let me remind you that you take your life into your hands when you touch a phone that is hanging upside down on the hook. This is the case when one of the BGF boys hung the phone upside down. A guy walked out of his cell and picked up the phone not knowing exactly what the meaning was when a phone is hanging upside down on a hook. The BGF boy walked up to the guy and said to the guy, "You know that is my phone that you are on?" The dude responded to the BGF boy, "Man can't you see me here on the phone?!" The BGF boy said, "Ok." He went back to his cell. Rec Hall time came. The BGF boy banged dude on the back of his head with the can of Mackerel. The other dude went down hard.

There were many other stabbings and other crimes and weapons used. Either I had seen them or I did them myself. These are just a few. The last and sixth weapon that I am going to talk about is the Baseball Bat. A bully asked a young guy to let him wear his sweat suit. The young man aloud the bully to do so. A week had gone by. One day, after the bully had come off his visit the young man asked him, "Can I get my sweat suit back?" The bully answered, "No!" The young man asked, "What, you plan on taking it?!" The bully replied, "Yes!" The young man said, "Oh, Ok!" But while the bully was in the Yard walking with a couple of guys who had the reputation of being a knife slinger, the young man waited patiently on the baseball field like he was waiting for the game to start. The bully, not thinking twice about the young man being there, just walked right pass him. Suddenly, there was a sound that could be heard all the way across the field; a sound like you would hear when a bat hit the ball out of the park. His two so-called friends stood there watching their buddy, the bully, get the beat down. This guy died twice from his beating, but was brought back to life both times. Another beating happened liked that over a gold chain. That beating ended in death.

SECTION II

TRANSITION FROM ISLAM TO CHRISTIANITY

• • •

IN SEARCH OF PEACE, I FOUND JESUS

...SOUGHT PEACE

CHAPTER 12

I accepted Islam with a heart filled with pain and a mind filled with confusion. I was searching for belonging, truth and significance. In my searching, I turned to religion. I looked to Islam. Years earlier, when I was just a child, my mother would occasionally take me to church. Although I attended church services, I was not a believer or follower of Jesus Christ. I did not have a set of religious values. I was neither saved nor baptized. In my formative years, my mother instructed me to tell people I was Catholic, should anyone ask. I was given a "name of a faith" but not "faith in a name." My parents did not tell me about God or who He was. They did not explain what it meant to be Catholic or the tenants of their professed faith. Yet, it seems, I always believed in a God. I spent many nights in prayer. I prayed more earnestly while I was in prison. I prayed for my freedom.

A good friend, Gary, introduced me to Islam. I endured so many fistfights, jailhouse brawls and knife fights with makeshift weapons. My friend confronted me in my reality, "Man! You are serving a life sentence. You are not going to make it in here if you don't get yourself together. You need to find some peace in your life. Otherwise, you are going to kill someone or someone is going to kill you." He was a Muslim. He believed Islam would provide the peace I so desperately needed. The problem was, I did not desire peace. I did not need peace. I wanted to continue a life of violence. My violence put the other inmates on notice - "I am not the one for your nonsense."

My friend's invitation to Islam seemed to motivate me. I eventually yielded and I accepted Islam as my new-found religion. I adopted the Islamic beliefs and patterned my life to the Islamic beliefs for the next fifteen (15) years. I elevated through the ranks of the organization. I was privileged to be assigned the position of security protection for the Imam. The Imam is the person who leads prayer in the mosque. I held that position for five (5) years. I protected the Imam, even with my life, if needed. I carried out every order, without question. I was faithfully loyal to the Imam. I was self-disciplined to pray five times each day at the appointed times.

My friend was right. I did find peace. Albeit, that peace was disrupted on several occasions when a non-Muslim threatened harm to a fellow Muslim brother or even to the Imam. Otherwise, Islam calmed my character, tremendously.

MUSLIMS WITH CHRISTIAN HEARTS

CHAPTER 13

I was a practicing Muslim for fifteen years, but I had the heart of a Christian. I was a stump down Muslim. I studied the faith and obeyed the teachings to the letter. I prayed five times a day. I fasted during Ramadan. I paid charity. I believed in God. However, because of my precarious predicament, I could never visit the Holy City of Mecca. In the Muslim faith, we were taught to believe in all gods, angels, books, prophets, and messengers. Yet, deep inside the recesses of my heart, there was a disturbance, a yearning, a clinging to the gospel of Jesus Christ.

I would reminisce and reflect on those days gone by. I could hear the gospel music that my mother used to play. The music filled my memory and it filled my heart. Yes! My heart was filled with gospel music, my mother's gospel music and love. I was so thankful. As strange as it seemed, it was like I had a connection to the Christian faith.

Sometimes I cried as I listened to old gospel music. It was as if the music found that sensitive spot in my heart. It was as if my heart was touched by Jesus Christ. At some point in my life Jesus had touched me. I was unaware of or insensitive to His touch, because Muslims believed in all gods. Reading books, including the Holy Bible's Old and New Testaments, was not only allowed, but encouraged. I took full advantage of that privilege. I read the Bible in my cell. Suddenly, the Bible resonated with me, as if it entered my soul. I incorporated listening to gospel music while I read the Bible. Reading the Christian Bible replaced reading the Quran. I memorized Biblical verses. My recitation of bible verses far outweighed recall of Quran passages. Although this was a radical change, something began to take place inwardly and outwardly. I was loyal to the Imam as his security officer. I faithfully served my position until the day I was released from prison on January 28, 2011. Like I mentioned before, I served 28 years, and one month.

I continued as a practicing Muslim for three more years even though I had the heart of a Christian. Afterwards, I began to attend church. Church attendance is a violation of Muslim faith. Muslims are not to enter the doors of a church. There is one exception warranting entrance into a Christian Church. This was to speak out against the pastor who proclaims Jesus Christ to be anything more than a prophet or messenger. At the same time my beautiful wife, Jamie was attending, The Ark Church, located in Odenton, Maryland. The Bishop along with other pastors at that church, at the time, had been praying for my release from prison. They had been diligently praying for a few years. When I finally met them, they confirmed what my wife had said was true.

I was thankful for the prayers that had been lifted

up to God on my behalf. I felt that the least I could do is visit this church to show my gratitude. While visiting there, I met a pastor unlike any other pastor. I mean, I kept a close eye on him, because I have met some false pastors before. They were dishonest and money hungry. I was also still maintaining my belief as a Muslim. But then I found myself in that very church crying, praying and praising the Lord; thanking my Lord and Savior for keeping me for 28 years and one month while I served in prison.

My co-defendant used to drive me and Jamie from Annapolis to Philly every Sunday. He really wanted me to come to his church and move to Philly, but God was really working on my heart there at the Ark Church in Anne Arundel County. The Lord earnestly spoke to my heart through Matthew 6:21, "For where your treasure is, there will your heart be also."[1] This Word of God rang out in my heart and mind. The peace and the heart of God spoke to me in Proverbs 3:5-6, "Trust in the Lord with all thine heart; and lean not unto thine own understanding. In all thy ways acknowledge him, and he shall direct thy paths."[2]

At the Ark Church, my heart and mind were being directed by the Lord to accept Christ, but it wasn't until the staff changed over. That is when God really deepened the need within my very spirit. God knew my heart. 1Kings 8:39 says, "Then hear thou in heaven thy dwelling place, and forgive, and do, and give to every man according to his ways, whose heart thou knowest; (for thou, even thou only, knowest the hearts of all the children of men)."[3] I placed my trust in Christ and disobeyed the command of Islam and continued going to church. I went on God's understanding, as He directed my feet to the path of acknowledgement in the Lord and who is our Savior. God knew that my prayer was to bring my heart and belief as ONE. God answers prayers and when you pray in His name, He will receive your prayer. This implies that when a person is seeking God, you are to pray in Jesus' Name. This means you HAVE accepted the Lord Jesus Christ as your Lord and Savior.

When the Bishop left, a new pastor, Bishop Antonio Palmer, took over the reins. He is a true example of a man. A man that is after God's heart. Not long after coming into his position, the church was moving and in dynamic direction. The name of the church was changed from the Ark Church to Kingdom Celebration Center. At that very time of changing hands and changing names, I accepted the Lord Jesus Christ; it was in 2014. My heart was then settled and at peace with the Lord. I became a full-blown Christian in heart and actions. Bishop Palmer and his wife, First Lady Barbara Palmer, can come with a powerful Word as well. They demonstrate their authentic leadership skills in love by teaching members the full panoramic of how to "love God, love people, and fulfill needs." On

January 1, 2015, the Bishop did a makeover on the entire church. That phrase became the goal of their mission statement.

Endnotes

1   Matthew 6:21 King James Version (KJV) Bible, [21] *For where your treasure is, there will your heart be also.*

2   Proverbs 3:5-6 King James Version (KJV) Bible, [5] *Trust in the Lord with all thine heart; and lean not unto thine own understanding.* [6] *In all thy ways acknowledge him, and he shall direct thy paths.*

3   1 Kings 8:39 King James Version (KJV) Bible, [39] *Then hear thou in heaven thy dwelling place, and forgive, and do, and give to every man according to his ways, whose heart thou knowest; (for thou, even thou only, knowest the hearts of all the children of men;)*

REJECTION OF THE MUSLIMS AS A CHRISTIAN

CHAPTER 14

After I became a Christian, my so-called friends began to slowly drop off like flies. As a Muslim, I had a lot of friends – hundreds of them. But now, they looked at me in disdain, as a disbeliever of Islam. I often felt the same way about them. They are disbelievers of Christianity. I told them I am committed to Christianity just as I was when I practiced Islam. "So back up. You be your way and I will be my way," is what I told them. I was also willing to protect my Bishop as I protected my Imam. So, make no mistakes here, I will fight for my leaders as well as my beliefs, if it came down to it. It is in the Word of God, **Hebrews 13:17**, *"Obey them that have the rule over you, and submit yourselves: for they watch for your souls, as they that must give account, that they may do it with joy, and not with grief: for that is unprofitable for you."*[1] So, with that in mind, I submit to my Bishop and First Lady Palmer, as well as the leaders there at Kingdom Celebration Center (KCC), giving them honor to their post.

It says in **Romans 10:9** that if thou shalt confess with thy mouth the Lord Jesus, and shalt believe in thine heart that God hath raised him from the dead, thou shalt be saved.[2] I truly believe in my heart that God saved and raised me up from the dead. I am saved and proud of it. I say that because Islam infected belief about Christianity. It is the one true faith and Christ is my Savior. I sometimes just think about how we were told to stay out of churches. Now I just think if I would have obeyed that simple command, I wouldn't have heard the Word of truth about deliverance and the salvation of my soul. I know that I chose to practice Islam to have peace, but in Christ I found a more complete and perfect peace. **Psalm 29:11** says, *"The Lord will give strength unto his people; the Lord will bless his people with peace."*[3] As a Muslim my heart was always a Christian. As a practicing Muslim I would call on God, but now all my prayers end in the Name of Jesus. **John 14:6** says, *"Jesus saith unto him, I am the way, the truth, and the life: no man cometh unto the Father, but by me."*[4] I believe that my having a Christian heart in prison and praying for my release is why God opened those gates after twenty-eight years and one month. God heard my prayers. **1 John 5:14** says, *"And this is the confidence that we have in him, that, if we ask any thing according to his will, he heareth us."*[5]

I was told by my Muslim friends that I was a *Kaffir*, which is an insulting term used by some Muslims for non-Muslims. Another word that they would use is an *Apostate*, meaning a person who renounces a religious or political belief or principle, i.e. a dissenter, defector, deserter, traitor, backslider, or turncoat. They are right in the aspect that I am a Christian that converted from Islam, but they are wrong that I don't have a belief. For I do believe in Jesus and He saved me and He is my

Lord and Savior.

Endnotes

1   Hebrews 13:17 King James Version (KJV) Bible, [17] *Obey them that have the rule over you, and submit yourselves: for they watch for your souls, as they that must give account, that they may do it with joy, and not with grief: for that is unprofitable for you.*

2   Romans 10:9 King James Version (KJV) Bible, [9] *That if thou shalt confess with thy mouth the Lord Jesus, and shalt believe in thine heart that God hath raised him from the dead, thou shalt be saved.*

3   Psalm 29:11 King James Version (KJV) Bible, [11] *The Lord will give strength unto his people; the Lord will bless his people with peace.*

4   John 14:6 King James Version (KJV) Bible, [6] *Jesus saith unto him, I am the way, the truth, and the life: no man cometh unto the Father, but by me.*

5   1 John 5:14 King James Version (KJV) Bible, [14] *And this is the confidence that we have in him, that, if we ask any thing according to his will, he heareth us.*

REPLACING THE QURAN SURAHS WITH BIBLE CHAPTERS AND VERSES

CHAPTER 15

After studying the Quran for so many years, learning of the Surahs germinated in my mind infecting the belief system. I started replacing them with scriptures from the Bible. I had to modify thoughts of religiosity that was prevalent in mind. In Islam, God is called by the Arabic name of Allah, which means "God." The difficulty was to reestablish the messengers and the prophets in my mind. The Quran and the Bible do not run parallel when it speaks on these. I began to study books of the Bible such as Matthew, Mark, Luke and John. These stories were presented by great men of the Bible who were infused by the Holy Spirit. I was in awe and honored them. It made a complete change in me to read the Word. The Islamic rendition of Jesus Christ had been debased to a mere messenger of God. But now my eyes and mind had been redeemed by the truth of the Word. I have learned the undeniable, controvertible truth.

Jesus, who is the Son of God, performed a number of miracles. Just to name a few out of the Bible:
- Jesus changes the water into wine. **John 2:1-11**
- Jesus cured the noble man's son, **John 2:46-53**
- Jesus fills the fishermen nets with fish, **Luke 5:1-11**
- Jesus cast out the unclean spirit, **Mark 1:23-27**
- Jesus cures Simon's mother-in-law of a fever,

Mark 1:30-31
- Jesus heals the Leper, **Mark 1:40-42**
- Jesus raised the widow's son from the dead, **Luke 7:12-15**

By my estimation you cannot call Jesus a mere messenger. Although He was indeed sent as a messenger to the world, He was truly the Son of God and our only Savior.

John 3:16 *"For God so loved the world, that he gave his only begotten Son, that whosoever believeth in him should not perish, but have everlasting life."*

Jesus is Lord and is exalted:

Philippians 2:9-11 *"Wherefore God also hath highly exalted him, and given him a name which is above every name: that at the name of Jesus every knee should bow, of things in heaven, and things in earth, and things under the earth; and that every tongue should confess that Jesus Christ is Lord, to the glory of God the Father."*

Jesus died for our sins so that we might have everlasting life:

Romans 5:8-10 *"But God commendeth his love toward us, in that, while we were yet sinners,*

Christ died for us. Much more then, being now justified by his blood, we shall be saved from wrath through him. For if, when we were enemies, we were reconciled to God by the death of his Son, much more, being reconciled, we shall be saved by his life."

I challenge anyone to try and state wrong provocation against my Lord and Savior who sacrificed His life for me and you. He was more than just a mere messenger. He was and is the Deliverer for all mankind.

My plans are to study the Bible just like I did with the Quran; to put every effort into every detail and receive the understanding, teaching and knowledge of the full doctrine of the Word. My hopes are to help educate other Muslim brothers and sisters to find clarification through my walk; that they might see the Christian God in me. I pray that their eyes and hearts be opened to the knowledge and full understanding of the Lord through the Word of God. The teachings of Islam are not of the God who I serve in Christianity.

There will be many Muslims who will want to know why I converted to Christianity. Christianity was already in my very spirit. I wanted to have a deeper relationship with God. As a Muslim, I was taught to stay away from churches and their services unless I was gainfully willing to go in and speak against the false teachings. Moreover, I should confront those leaders of Christianity and dispute against Jesus being the Son of God. I could not, because I know who Jesus is in my spirit. Down in my soul, I heard a voice speaking to me that there was more. The Bible teaches us in **1 John 4:10,** *"Herein is love, not that we loved God, but that he loved us, and sent his Son to be the propitiation for our sins."*

We can find so many books and verses that give impervious doctrine that Jesus is Lord. Just think, if I never came to Kingdom Celebration Center, I would not have been thoroughly introduced to the Word of God. I would not have been delivered and set free.

The problem with Muslim doctrine is this: as their article of faith, the Bible is not excluded but included. As a Muslim you are to believe in all of God's Books, including the Old and New Testament. That's the Muslim doctrine. There six articles of faith, which is the fundamental base to the Muslim belief system, states that every Muslim must ascribe to these set beliefs. The six Articles of Faith is why I needed to mollify myself. I started reading the Bible because I needed to find answers for the questions I had in my mind, heart, spirit and soul. The Muslim doctrine was not doing that for me. I believe that when I started reading the Bible, it created a Christian heart in me. I will preach and teach the true Word of God to my friends and let their hearts be changed to the Word of God in Christianity.

THREE REASONS FOR MY CONVERSION

CHAPTER 16

Reason #1
A Christian Heart

I practiced Islam for over 15 years during my prison journey, but I had a Christian heart and belief, and prayed that God would sincerely release me from my bondage. Even though my faith was that of a mustard seed (Luke 17:6), it was better than having no faith at all. I would pray to God faithfully, never once labeling Jesus as a mere messenger. I sincerely believed that God would vindicate me and open those prison gates for me. I realized later that He did in fact open those gates for me, not in my time, but in His. I needed time there to serve, develop and grow. So, God's timing was twenty-eight years and one month.

Reason #2
Jesus Gave me Peace

In chapter 12 of this book, I told you about a buddy of mine that introduced me to Islam because of my bad attitude and conduct. I was rampant and violent. I needed peace in my life. Therefore, I accepted Islam into my life. The peace they sold me on was counterfeit and fraudulent. Even with Islam, when I was moved up in ranks and protected the Imam, I still was confronted with violence from others in the prison. The Muslims created beefs with the gangs causing ongoing opposition. There was no genuine peace. However, when I found Jesus, who is peace, I became saved and protected under His blood. He left me with His peace.

> **John 14:27** *"Peace I leave with you, my peace I give unto you: not as the world giveth, give I unto you. Let not your heart be troubled, neither let it be afraid."*

> **John 16:33** *"These things I have spoken unto you, that in me ye might have peace. In the world ye shall have tribulation: but be of good cheer; I have overcome the world."*

I read these passages of the Bible over and over again before being saved. Even when I was released from prison, I had found that this world was not peaceful at all and I needed to stay grounded. I read these scriptures to remind me who Jesus was and is; they brought me peace. In this world we need peace. The peace that God brings is not absent from troubles, but it is the calm in the middle of turbulent and trying times. It is a peace that guides you to a place in God, such as that of Paul and Silas (Acts 16:25).

Reason #3
In Islam God Says Believe in the Bible

When I was a Muslim, I was taught by leaders not to read the Bible because it was tampered with or distorted. But the infraction with this was that God tells the Muslim, as the six Articles of Faith would have it, to believe in all Books of the Bible, which includes the New and the Old Testament thereof.

These are my three logical reasons of why I converted from Islam to Christianity. I invite my Muslim friends to come and accept Christ as your Lord and Savior. I speak to the same brothers that love me; those who are willing to give their own life for me as I would do for them.

Surely, I am under a man of God that has integrity and valor. Bishop Antonio Palmer is not a man who embezzles or plunders from the church or congregants. He is like us, a strong soldier in the street. But he is an ambassador for Jesus. He works hard for his family and is not afraid of work itself. He is not a man of extravagance, having to own large mansions, fancy cars and diamond rings. This is not who he is. He is about the people and bringing them to the truth of God, teaching Kingdom principles under the sound doctrine of Jesus Christ. Most importantly, saving souls and helping communities grow under the covering of an open heaven is what he is about – the Father's business. He is truly endowed by the Holy Spirit. This is what makes Bishop Antonio Palmer who he is to me – someone that I value and respect.

There is one other nugget I wanted to share with you and wanted you to roll this thing around in your head. Consider this food for thought. This was another reason that enlightened me to convert to Christianity.

The Holy Quran states:

> **Surah 5:44** *"Indeed, We sent down the Torah, in which was guidance and light."*
>
> **Surah 5:46** *"And We sent, following in their footsteps, Jesus, the son of Mary, confirming that which came before him in the Torah; and We gave him the Gospel, in which was guidance and light and confirming that which preceded it of the Torah as guidance and instruction for the righteous."*

This is in the Holy Quran. I need you to read this and know that I have done the same.

HOW GOD KEPT ME

CHAPTER 17

I can truly say that God sent His angels to place a hedge of protection around me. He didn't have to keep me, but he did. I am grateful for what He did for me and who He is in my life today. On many occasions, I should have died, but the Lord God saved me. From the pit of my own hellish ways, He saved me. Just to name a few occasions, read it and you be the judge.

In 1979, I was shot at, as I was running through some woods. I could hear the bullets flying past me hitting the trees. Thank God I didn't get hit.

In 1981, I was again shot at by some Jamaicans, who really had it in for me and wanted to do some deadly harm. Again, the bullets flew past my head hitting the dirt of the hill as I was running up the hill.

In 1982, I was incarcerated and told that I was to serve a death penalty. They were seeking to take my life, but God said, "NOT SO!" and did not let it happen. He told me not to worry and I didn't. He removed the penalty.

Then, God, out of his profound grace and mercy, saw me through 10,334 days of incarceration. He placed a hedge of protection around me, not allowing any physical harm to my body. I was in several knife fights and was never stabbed – not even once! Not one cut or scratch in any of these battles. I am not bragging on these actual attacks. I am talking about the miracles of God. He sent His holy angels to surround me and protect me from all harm. This is one of the reasons why I praise Him. I lift Him up. I give Him the honor that is due His precious name.

Even when the parole officers and agents on numerous attempts tried to add more time onto my parole, the Lord would lower my time even more. God even lowered my time so low that I had almost no time to have to serve parole. Thank you, Jesus. I am at a point now where I no longer serve any supervised parole. This is the most freedom I have had since December 24, 1982. Praise the Lord! It is my 7th Anniversary since I have been released from prison. The Lord provided me with a job one month after my release. I have four sons and four grandchildren, plus a beautiful wife that I adore and is my helpmate who keeps this all together for Jesus.

In 2009, I lost my parents while I was incarcerated. Their deaths were two months apart from one another. They would not allow me to attend either of the funerals. God brought me through all that and He held me and helped me to make it through the hard times. He continues to help me, as I will continue to serve Him no matter what. He is my deliverer and the healer of my very soul. He has made me understand that EVERY DAY MUST COUNT. I serve Him for life. I hope this book and testimony inspires you to serve Him for life, too. May His unmerited grace be upon you.

www.ingramcontent.com/pod-product-compliance
Lightning Source LLC
Chambersburg PA
CBHW052200110526
44591CB00012B/2022